J. V. Read

Beginner's Manual for Bible study

J. V. Read

Beginner's Manual for Bible study

ISBN/EAN: 9783337171612

Printed in Europe, USA, Canada, Australia, Japan

Cover: Foto ©ninafisch / pixelio.de

More available books at **www.hansebooks.com**

FOR

BIBLE STUDY

OR HINTS AS TO

WHAT THE BIBLE IS

AND HOW TO USE IT IN

PERSONAL WORK.

Compiled by J. V. READ.

CHICAGO:
YOUNG MEN'S ERA PUBLISHING CO.
1891.

PREFACE.

Many young people, and many new converts, really desire to be soul-winners, but shrink from all effort in the direction of personal work because of a consciousness of not knowing how to proceed. The "Sword of the Spirit" is recognized as the one effective weapon for aggressive warfare and one of the hopeful signs of the times is the large number of " Workers' Training Classes " which are giving to their members a knowledge of how to use the Word of God. Of the several outlines of study for such classes which have been published, all, or nearly all, are better suited to the use of those who are somewhat advanced in Bible Study, and a desire for something that should be specially adapted to beginners has led to the compilation of this little Manual, which makes no claim to be anything more than a gathering up of such outlines and suggestions as have been demonstrated by experience to be practical in giving instruction as to what the Bible is, what it teaches, and how to use it in personal work. The course is elementary and fundamental, making a basis that will be of great value for the deeper study of the Scriptures in later years. The compiler has found that beginners are more easily interested in the study of persons than of book outlines or topics, and it is therefore expected that the consideration of the characters of the Bible, in such connection with chronology as makes their position in history easily recalled, will give such utility to the course as to make it desirable.

In organizing a Bible Training Class, a few things are very important:

1. The class should not be large. Greater freedom and best results are secured in a class of six to ten members. In no case should there be more than twelve to sixteen. If a greater number apply, organize more classes.

2. The members of the class should be only those who will concede that a knowledge of the Scriptures is as important to spiritual life as a common school education is to social life, and who will manifest an earnestness in securing this knowledge.

3. A pledge should be signed, binding each (a) to be present at each session of the class (sickness, absence from the city, or previous permission of the leader alone excusing) and (b) to spend not less than one hour per week in diligent study preparatory to the study of the class room. Some classes make the limit two or even three hours.

4 The hour for the class should be the most convenient in the week for those who are members; the room should be not large but well ventilated, free from interruption, provided with a large table or tables and a blackboard if possible.

5. Each member of the class should possess a good reference Bible, Smith's Bible Dictionary, Index to the Bible, Cruden's Concordance, and a cheap note book with lead pencil. The Bible and note book should always be brought to the class room.

6. Personal work should be at once commenced by the members of the class. Only thus can they get the full benefit of the course of study. All theory is of but little value without practice. The earlier we begin, the more time will we have in which to honor our Lord.

CONTENTS.—Part I.

HOLY SCRIPTURES.

CONTENTS.—Part 2.

USE OF THE SCRIPTURES.

LESSON I.

PART I.—THE BIBLE.

A wonderful book written by about thirty-five men—ranking from humblest herdsmen to most wise scholars and kings—and covering 1,600 years of time, but dictated by the Triune God to show mankind the way to be saved from sin.

Suppose the figure 3 to represent the Trinity.

Set down this figure (3) and next to it its square (9) and we have the number of books in the Old Testament. } 39

Multiply these two figures (3 and 9) together and we get the number of books in the New Testament. } 27

Books in both Testaments, 66

As if the 3 were doubled for emphasis and marked down for each Testament. Thus the matters pertaining to the Trinity pervade both Testaments.

Learn the names of the books of the Old Testament and be able to recite them in order.

PART 2.—HOW TO STUDY THE BIBLE.

We are to understand that it is *infallible*,
Isaiah viii, 20.

Because God says so. II Pet. i, 21.

Because the Old Testament was so care-
fully guarded and handed down by the
Jews—from Moses on through the rulers to
Ezra, the Rabbis, etc.

Because the Old and New Testaments
have been preserved and copied by monks
and hermits in monasteries, etc., to the
time of the printing press.

NOTES ON LESSON I.

LESSON II.

PART I.—TITLES OF THE BIBLE.

Commonly used—
Bible, Book of Books, Inspired Word, Holy Writ.

Found in the Bible—
The Book, Book of the Law, Book of the Covenant, Law of the Lord, Law and the Prophets, Moses and the Prophets, The Scriptures, Holy Scriptures, The Word, Word of God, Word of Christ.

(*Figurative.*)   Fire, Hammer, Lamp, Milk, Meat, Seed, Sword.

Which of these titles refer to the entire Bible, and which to only a part of it?

Locate Places in the Bible where those are to be found which refer to the entire Bible.

Which one do you prefer? and why?

Learn names of the books of the New Testament and be able to recite them in order.

PART 2.—HOW TO STUDY THE BIBLE.

(1) That we may understand the *way of Salvation.* John xx, 31, and

(2) That we may grow spiritually. II Pet. ii, 2.

In order to accomplish these things to best advantage, the study must be done:

(a) *Prayerfully,* Eph. vi, 18 (first clause).

(b) *Daily,* Job. xxiii, 12 (last clause).

NOTES ON LESSON II.

LESSON III.

(1) Pentateuch—5—G. E. L. N. D.

(2) Historical—12— $\begin{cases} \text{J. J. R.} \\ \text{}^1\text{S. }^2\text{S. }^1\text{K. }^2\text{K. }^1\text{C. }^2\text{C.} \\ \text{E. N. E.} \end{cases}$

(3) Poetic—5—J. P. P. E. SS.

(4) Prophetic $\begin{cases} \text{Greater—5—I. J. L. E. D.} \\ \text{Lesser-12} \begin{cases} \text{Ho. Jo. Am.} \\ \text{Ob. Jo. Mi. Na.} \\ \text{Ha. Ze. Ha. Ze. Ma.} \end{cases} \end{cases}$

Drill in finding them.

PART 2.—WHAT THE BIBLE TEACHES.

(1) *About Salvation:*
  (a) Everybody needs it, Rom. iii, 22, 23.
  (b) God wants all to have it,
                    Ezek. xviii, 32.
  (c) It is through Christ only, Acts. iv, 12.

(2) *About Growth in Grace:*
  (a) It is expected, II Peter iii, 18.
  (b) It is gradual, Mark iv. 28.
  (c) It is through life in Christ, John xv, 4.

NOTES ON LESSON III.

LESSON IV.

Historical—5—M. M. L. J. A.

Epistolary {

Pauline—14 { R. ¹C. ²C. G. E. P. C. ¹T. ²T. ¹T. ²T. T. P. H.

General—7 { J. ¹P. ²P. ¹J. ²J. ³J. J.

Prophetic—1—Rev.

Drill in finding them.

PART 2.—WHAT THE BIBLE TEACHES ABOUT
GOD.

(a) He is eternal, Deut. xxxii, 40.
(b) He is One, yet three persons,
          Deut. vi, 4; Matt. iii, 16, 17.
(c) He is almighty, Gen. i, 1.
(d) He is holy, Lev. xix, 2.
(e) He is merciful and just, Ex. xxxiv, 7.

———

NOTES ON LESSON IV.

LESSON V.

PART I.—OUTLINE FOR STUDY OF THE OLD TESTAMENT BY CHARACTERS.

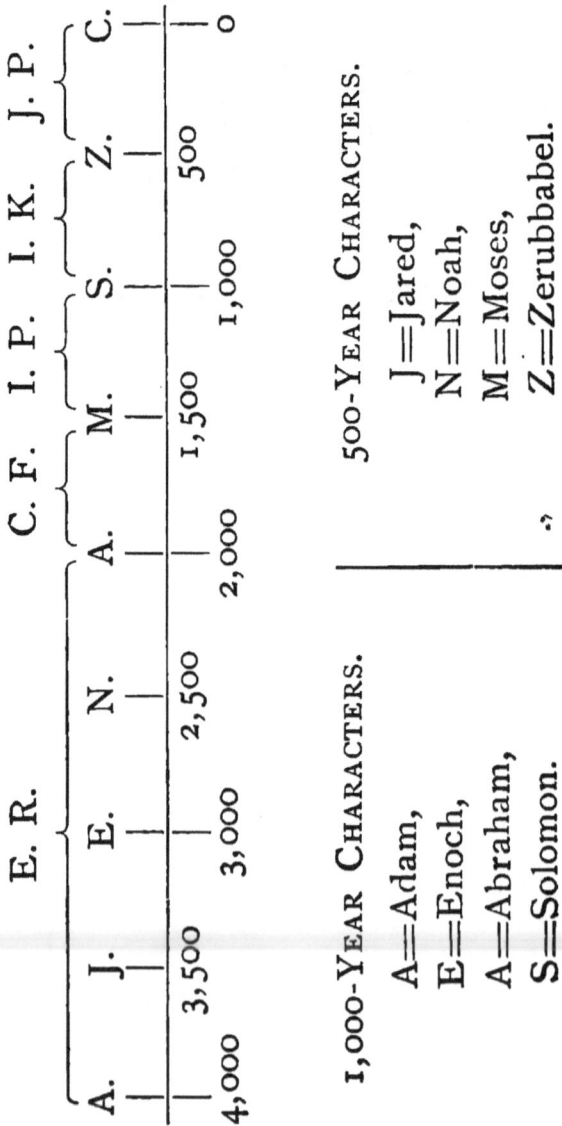

```
A.   J.   E.   N.   A.   M.   S.   Z.   C.
                E. R.        C. F.  I. P.  I. K.  J. P.

4,000  3,500  3,000  2,500  2,000  1,500  1,000  500  0
```

1,000-YEAR CHARACTERS.

A=Adam,
E=Enoch,
A=Abraham,
S=Solomon.

500-YEAR CHARACTERS.

J=Jared,
N=Noah,
M=Moses,
Z=Zerubbabel.

EXPLANATION OF DIAGRAM.

The straight line in diagram indicates the time from Adam to Christ divided into periods of 1,000 years, with subdivisions of 500 years, each period finding on the scene some prominent character of Bible History.

Curved lines indicate the General Periods of Bible History as follows: E. R. =Early Races; C. F. =Chosen Family; I. P. = Israel as a People; I. K. =Israel as a Kingdom; J. P. =The Jewish Province.

Thorough knowledge of these will greatly simplify Bible study.

PART 2.—WHAT THE BIBLE TEACHES ABOUT CHRIST.

(a) He is like unto us, Phil. ii, 7.
(b) He is Divine, Matt. iii, 17.
(c) He is our Saviour, I Tim. i, 15.
(d) He is our Life, I Jno. v, 11.

NOTES ON LESSON V.

LESSON VI.

PART I.—THE HISTORY OF ADAM.

Gen. i, 26 to v, 5.

Meaning of name.   Earthy Man.

Probably thus named because of his origin.

His Start in Life.
In the image of God, i, 27.
With good surroundings,
i, 28, 29, and ii, 8-12.
With only one restriction, ii, 17.
His Companion.
Intended as a helper, ii, 18.
Goes wrong and leads him astray, iii, 6.
His Later Life.
Banished under curse, iii, 16-24.
Sorrow, Thorns, Sweat.
Children given, iv, 1, 2, 25.
Cain, Abel, Seth.
Death—aged 930 years, v, 5.

PRACTICAL THOUGHTS.

Opportunities with great possibilities,
Matt. xxv, 29.
Influence of companionship, Ps. i, 1.
Deliverance from the curse,
Gen. iii, 15; II Pet. iii, 13.

Through
Sorrow, Matt. xxvi, 38.
Sweat, Luke, xxii, 44.
Thorns, John, xix, 5.

PART 2.—WHAT THE BIBLE TEACHES ABOUT
THE HOLY SPIRIT.

(a) He is a person, Acts xiii, 2.
(b) He is divine, I Pet. i, 12.
(c) His work is to convert, Tit. iii, 5.
(d) After conversion,
> He leads, Rom. viii, 14.
> Comforts, Jno. xiv, 16.
> Gives power, Acts i, 8.

NOTES ON LESSON VI.

LESSON VII.

JARED,—Gen. v, 15-20.

Meaning of name, Descent.

Patriarch—fifth from Adam.

Born 3544 B. C.   Died 2582 B. C.

Name seemingly recorded, with nine others in the same chapter, to trace the line of descent and show the long life of the patriarchs who were probably worshippers of God.

ENOCH,—Gen. v. 18-24.

Meaning of name, Experienced.

Patriarch—son of Jared and father of Methuselah, the two oldest men that ever lived.   Born?——   Died?——

Contemporary with all the preceding patriots, also with polygamous Lamech whose son Jabal was the first herdsman, Jubal, inventor of musical instruments and Tubal Cain the first smith.

He prophesied against the evils of his day, Jude, 14, 15.

He walked with God, Gen. v, 22, 24.

He pleased God, Heb. xi, 5.

PRACTICAL THOUGHTS.

True religion brings long life and happiness, Prov. iii, 1, 2.

To walk with God is better than the enjoyment of the world, Ps. lxiii, 3.

PART 2.—WHAT THE BIBLE TEACHES ABOUT
REGENERATION.

(a) It is necessary, John iii, 3, 7.
(b) It is a partaking of the divine nature,
II Pet. i, 4.
(c) It is a work of the Holy Spirit,
Titus iii, 5.
(d) It comes through the word,
I Pet. i, 23.
(e) It is brought about by faith,
I John v, 1.

NOTES ON LESSON VII.

LESSON VIII.

PART I.—THE HISTORY OF NOAH.

Gen. v, 29 to ix, 29.

Meaning of name, Rest or Comfort.

Before the Flood.
Bad surroundings, Gen. vi, 5.
A faithful preacher,
Gen. vi, 9; II Pet. ii, 5.
Builder of the Ark, Gen. vi, 22.

During the Flood.
The Ark filled, Gen, vii, 19.
Rain, high water, Gen. vii, 12-24.
Ark rests on Ararat, Gen. viii, 4.

After the Flood.
The first Altar and Sacrifice,
Gen, viii, 20.
The Covenant, Gen. ix, 8-17.
Death, aged 950, Gen. ix, 29.

PRACTICAL THOUGHTS.

In the world but not of it, John xvii, 15.
Safety under God's care, Psa. xci, 9, 10.
Sacrifice pleasing to God, Rom. xii, 1.

PART I.—WHAT THE BIBLE TEACHES ABOUT
FAITH.

(a) It is assurance, Heb. xi, 1.   (R. V.)
(b) It is believing God, Heb, xi, 6.
(c) It is receiving Christ, John i, 12.
(d) It is committing all to Christ,
Isa. xxvi, 3.

NOTES ON LESSON VIII.

.

LESSON IX.

PART I.—THE HISTORY OF ABRAHAM.

Gen. xi, 25, to xxv, 10.

Meaning of name, Father of a multitude.

Family Record.

Born in Ur of Chaldees, Gen. xi, 28.

Son of Terah, Uncle of Lot, Gen. xi, 27.

Father of Ishmael and Isaac,
    Gen. xvi, 15, and xxi, 3.

Incidents in His Life.

Moves to Haran, Father dies,
    Gen. xi, 31, 32.

Moves to Canaan, receives the promise, erects an altar, Gen. xii, 5-8.

Moves to Egypt, deceives Pharaoh, is banished and returns to Canaan,
    Gen. xii, 10, and xiii, 1.

Separation from Lot, Gen. xiii, 9.

Rescues Lot from Captors,
    Gen. xiv, 1-16.

Circumcision and Promise, Gen. xvii, 10.

Destruction of Sodom, Gen. xix, 24, 25.

Deceit at Gerar, Gen. xx, 2.

Offering of Isaac, Gen. xxii, 1-14.

PRACTICAL THOUGHTS.

Dangers of Worldly Prosperity,
    Matt. xiii, 22.

Reward of Unselfishness, Luke vi, 38.

Power of Faith, Rom. iv, 20-22.

PART 2.—WHAT THE BIBLE TEACHES ABOUT
CONFESSION.

(a) It is necessary, Matt. x, 32-33.
(b) It involves testifying by mouth,
Rom. x, 9.
(c) It demands church membership,
Matt. iii, 15; Luke xxii, 19.
(d) It requires a consistent Christian life,
I Pet. ii, 9.

NOTES ON LESSON IX.

LESSON X.

PART I.—THE HISTORY OF MOSES.

Meaning of name, Saved from the Water.

Forty years; Educational,
Ex. ii, 1-15; Acts vii, 20-29.
Born, Hidden, Found.
Advantages of a Prince.
Defends an Israelite; compelled to flee.

Forty years; Preparatory,
Ex. ii, 21—iv, 31; Acts vii, 29-35.
Service in Midian; Marriage.
Revelation through Burning Bush.
Return to Egypt with Aaron.

Forty years; Active Work of Life,
Leads Israel forth: *Exodus.*
10 plagues, v-xii; Miracles, xiv-xvii.
Law at Sinai, xix-xxiii; Golden Calf, xxxii;
Tabernacle.
Guide through wanderings: *Numbers.*
Smites the Rock, xx, 7-12.
Dies at Mt. Nebo,
Deut. xxxii, 49, 50; xxxiv, 5, 6.

PRACTICAL THOUGHTS.

Proper education must have Piety for a foundation, Prov. ix, 10.
Communion with God the best preparation for life, Ps. cxix, 72.
The power of a consecrated life,
Phil. iv, 13.

PART 2.—HOW TO USE THE BIBLE IN PERSONAL WORK.

1. *Know* that *you* are saved, and *how;*
Titus iii, 5.

2. Realize that you are not opening a matter for discussion but dealing with a *settled fact*, John iii, 18.

3. Remember that each inquirer has *one chief* difficulty. Find it and remove it.

4. *Never* engage in a controversy. If any candid objections appear, answer them, not with arguments or somebody's experience, but with the Word of God.

5. Understand that nowhere in the Bible does *feeling* appear as a condition or element of salvation. Teach *faith.*

6. Gently but earnestly urge *immediate* decision. It may be the *last* opportunity of the inquirer—or yourself.

7. Be prayerful. Use tact. Depend on the *Holy Spirit* for power to convert.

8. Study your Bible *every day* and be familiar with at least one passage for each of the different classes of people that you are likely to meet.

NOTES ON LESSON **X.**

LESSON XI.

PART I.—HISTORY OF SOLOMON.

Meaning of name, Peaceable.

Early Surroundings.
Kingdom of David, I Chr. xxii, 7, 8.
Conspiracy of Absalom,
          II Sam. xv, 1—xviii, 17.
Conspiracy of Adonijah, I Kin. i, 5-53.

Prime of Life.
Choice of Wisdom, I Kin. iii, 5-14.
The temple, I Kin. vi, 1-9.
Magnificent reign, I Kin. x, 4-7;
    political alliances; splendor of court;
Song of Solomon; Proverbs.

Later Years.
Oppression of Israelites, I Kin. xii, 1-4.
Enslaving of Canaanites,
          II Chr. ii, 17, 18.
Strange women, idolatry; II Kin. xi, 1-11;
    Ecclesiastes (?).

PRACTICAL THOUGHTS.

A wise son the hope of the family,
          Prov. xv, 20.
We get what we choose, Matt. vii, 7.
The world powerless to satisfy,
          Eccl. ii, 11.

PART 2.—DEALING WITH ONE WHO DON'T KNOW WHETHER HE IS A CHRISTIAN.

Show him that his attitude toward Christ determines it (John iii, 18).

That God's Word is to turn his belief into positive knowledge (I John v, 13).

That this assurance is to come through trusting (Isa. l, 10), and following the Lord (John viii, 12).

That love for Christians will be one of the vidences (I John iii, 14).

———

NOTES ON LESSON XI.

LESSON XII.

PART I.—HISTORY OF ZERUBBABEL.

Meaning of name, Stranger at Babylon.

His Surroundings.

Israel in Captivity, Jerusalem destroyed,
Temple burned, II Chr. xxxvi, 14-21.
Cyrus Liberates the Captives,
Ezra i, 1-3.
The Return—Zerubbabel as leader,
Ezra i, 5—ii, 67.

Incidents in His Work.

Feasts, Sacrifice and Praise, Ez. iii.
Temple building, Opposition, and 16
years' delay, Ez. iv.
Revival under the Prophets, Ez. v, 1, 2.
Opposition brings help, Ez. v, 3—vi, 13.
Completion of Temple and rejoicing,
Ez. vi, 14-22.

PRACTICAL THOUGHTS.

Rulers of Nations in God's hand,
Prov. xxi, 1.
When God helps all goes well,
Phil. v. 19.

PART 2.—DEALING WITH ONE WHO WILL NOT
BECOME A CHRISTIAN BECAUSE HE FEARS
THAT OTHERS WILL LAUGH AT HIM.

Show him that he lacks manly spirit,
                              I Peter iii, 13.
That he lacks wisdom also,
                    Luke xii, 4, 5; Matt. v, 10.

NOTES ON LESSON XII.

LESSON XIII.

PART I.—THE HISTORY OF JESUS CHRIST.

Meaning of name, Anointed Saviour.

(a) The Period of His Preparation.

Birth and Infancy.
The Annunciation, Luke i, 26-33.
Song of Mary—Song of Zacharias.
Birth at Bethlehem, Luke ii, 1-7.
Taxing of Parents, Manger at Inn.
First Visitors, Luke ii, 8-40; Matt. ii,
1-11—Shepherds—Simeon and Anna
—Wise Men.

Preservation and Boyhood.
Flight to Egypt, Matt. ii, 13-18.
Herod's decree.
Return to Nazareth, Matt. ii, 19-23.
Herod's death.
Visit to Jerusalem, Luke ii, 41-52.
Passover—Lost from Parents.

Ripenings of Manhood.
The Forerunner, Luke, iii, 1-18.
Preaching—Baptizing.
The Baptism, Matt. iii, 13-17.
In Jordan—To fulfill righteousness.
The Great Temptation, Matt. iv, 1-11.
Appetite—Presumption—Ambition.

PRACTICAL THOUGHTS.

Prophecy will all be fulfilled, Matt. v, 18.
Obedience brings divine protection and
blessing, Deut. xi, 13-16.

PART 2.—DEALING WITH ONE WHO WOULD
RATHER PLAY BALL OR SKATE ON SUNDAY
THAN ATTEND THE MEETING.

Show him that the pleasure of the wicked
is short lived and don't pay, Eccl. xi, 9;
Isa. lviii, 13, 14; Mark viii, 36.
Don't associate with him very much,
II Tim. iii, 4, 5; Ps. i, 1.

NOTES ON LESSON XIII.

LESSON XIV.

PART I.—THE HISTORY OF JESUS CHRIST.
(b) His Work and Methods.

His Teaching.

By Pictures:—The New Birth—The Vine
—The Lily, John iii, 3; Jno. xv, 5;
Matt. vi, 28.

By Parables:—The Backslider—The
Christian Worker—Reward and Pun-
ishment, Luke xv, 11-24, Luke x,
30-37; Luke xvi, 19-31.

By Proverbs:—On Mount—On Plain—In-
cidentally, Matt. v, 1-10; Luke vi, 27,
28; Mark ii, 27.

His Miracles.

On Man:—Disease Healed—Demons
cast out—Dead raised, Mark i, 40-45;
Mark i, 21-28; Luke vii, 11-17.

On Nature:—Changing—Controlling—
Multiplying, John ii, 1-11; Mark iv,
35-41; Mark vi, 35-44.

The Apostolate Formed.

Twelve Humble Men:—Teaching—Work-
ing Miracles, Mark iii, 14-19.

Patient Training:—Doctrine—Personal
Influence; Luke xi, 1-13; John xiii, 15.

Full Commission:—World-wide—With
power, Matt. xxviii, 19, 20; Acts i, 8.

PRACTICAL THOUGHTS.

The power of pure speech, Prov. xxv, 11.
The Christian a wonder-worker,

Jno. xiv, 12; Matt. xxi, 21.
Christianity to be perpetuated,

II Tim. ii, 2.

PART 2.—DEALING WITH THE CHRISTIAN WHO HAS STOPPED ATTENDING THE MEETINGS.

He is probably allowing worldly things to gain his affections, Matt. vi, 21.
. This displeases God, Rev. ii, 4.
It endangers his spiritual life,
Ex. xxiii, 32, 33.

NOTES ON LESSON XIV,

LESSON XV.

PART I.—HISTORY OF JESUS CHRIST.

(c) His Passion.

Opposition.

From Pharisees, Luke xi, 53, 54—Pre-judices crossed—Hypocrisy Unveiled.

From Sadduces and Herodians, Matt. xxii, 16-33—Political revolt feared.

Trial.

Before Annas, Jno. xviii, 13, 14—Preceded by Agony, Betrayal and Arrest.

Before Caiaphas and Sanhedrim, Mark xiv, 53-65—Night—False witnesses—Buffeting.

Before Pilate, Luke xxiii, 1-15—Acquittal—Return from Herod, robed—Given over to mob.

Death.

On the Cross, Matt. xxvii, 35.

After scourging and mockery.

The Crowd, Matt. xxvii, 41, 54-56.

Jews, Soldiers, Women.

Last Words—Seven sentences. Repeat them.

PRACTICAL THOUGHTS.

Christ's followers may expect opposition.

Jno. xv, 20.

Trials bring fellowship with Christ,

1 Pet. iv, 12, 13.

Christ's death that we may have life,

1 Pet. ii, 24.

PART 2.—DEALING WITH ONE WHO "WILL BECOME A CHRISTIAN SOME OTHER TIME."

Show him that it is not certain that he will ever reach that time, Prov. xxvii, 1.

If he does reach the time in his mind he will be farther away from God and less likely to listen to the Holy Spirit than now. God's word either makes tender or hardens, Deut. xi, 26-28.

NOTES ON LESSON XV.

LESSON XVI.

PART I.—PERIODS OF THE HUMAN RACE.

(1) The Early Races, Adam to Abraham.

God deals. with the race, or races, direct.

(a) In Innocency.
In Eden, Gen. ii, 8.
One command as law, Gen. ii, 17.
Transgression, driving forth,
Gen. iii, 6-24.

(b) Under Conscience.
Fresh start outside of Eden, Gen. iv.
Gigantic failure, Gen. vi, 5-7.
The deluge, Gen. vii, 19-22.

(c) Under ties of Brotherhood.
Another trial after the Flood, Gen. ix, 1-3.
The Covenant promise, Gen. ix, 8-13.
Distrust of God, Babel, Gen. xi, 4-9.

PRACTICAL THOUGHTS.

Splendid surroundings not a reliable safeguard, Rom. i, 21.
Conscience unsafe unless regenerated,
Acts viii, 3; Jno. iii, 7.
"Brotherhood of Man" not sufficient to give eternal life, Mark x, 21.

PART 2.—DEALING WITH ONE WHO WOULD
LIKE TO BECOME A CHRISTIAN, BUT
DON'T KNOW HOW.

He must have such a sorrow for his sin
as will lead him to forsake it,

2 Cor. vii, 10.

He must accept Jesus Christ as his personal Saviour, John i, 12.

He must confess Him before men,

Rom. x, 9.

He must decide to follow Him through
life, John viii, 12.

NOTES ON LESSON XVI.

LESSON XVII.

PART I.—PERIODS OF THE HUMAN RACE.

(2) The chosen family—Abraham to Moses.

God deals with the race as connected with the chosen family.

Principal Characters:
Abraham, Lot, Isaac, Jacob, Esau, Joseph.

Sevenfold Promise to Abraham,
Gen. xii, 2, 3.
Make of him a great nation. Bless him. Make his name great. Make him a blessing. Bless his friends. Overthrow his enemies. Bless all the earth in him.

Prominent Events.
Covenant with Abraham, Gen. xv, 5-21.
Destruction of Sodom, Gen. xix, 17-26.
Offering of Isaac, Gen. xxii, 1-14.
Guile of Jacob, Gen. xxvii, 18-23.
Guile of Jacob's sons, Gen. xxxvii, 12-34.
Canaan deserted for Egypt,
Gen. xlvii, 28; Gen. l, 22, 26.

PRACTICAL THOUGHTS.

The righteous man always blessed,
Ps. v, 12.
The patience of a covenant-keeping God with covenant-breaking men, Jer. iii, 14.

PART 2.—DEALING WITH ONE WHO HAS DE-
CIDED TO TRY TO DO BETTER, BUT IS NOT
WILLING TO CONFESS CHRIST.

Show him that good deeds cannot save
him, Isa. lxiv, 6; James ii, 10.

He cannot be saved without confessing
Christ, Matt. x, 32, 33; Rom. x, 10.

NOTES ON LESSON XVII.

LESSON XVIII.

PART I.—PERIODS OF THE HUMAN RACE.

(3) Israel as a People—Moses to Saul.

God deals with His people through leaders chosen by Himself.

Under Moses.
Great Deliverance, *Exodus.*
Ten Plagues; Signs and Wonders.
Wilderness Wanderings, *Numbers.*
Murmurings; Wants supplied.
A Complete Law, *Deuteronomy.*
Religious; Sanitary; Political.

Under Joshua.
Canaan entered, Josh. iii, 9-17.
Enemies conquered, Josh. xi, 18-22.
Land divided, Josh. xiv, 1-5.

Under Judges.
Backsliding and deliverances,
Judg. ii, 11-16.
Great degeneracy, Judg. ii, 19, 20.
Clamor for a king, I Sam. viii, 19-22.

PRACTICAL THOUGHTS.

The insufficiency of a perfect law,
Acts xiii, 39.
Diligence always rewarded,
Luke xix, 16, 17,
Folly of trust in man, Ps. cxviii, 9.

PART 2.—DEALING WITH ONE WHO WILL NOT
BECOME A CHRISTIAN BECAUSE HE FEARS
THAT "HE WILL NOT HOLD OUT."

He is not "holding out" now, Eph. ii, 12.
The Christ who saves the soul will keep
it, Phil. i, 6; I Cor. x, 13; Phil. iv. 19.

NOTES ON LESSON XVIII.

LESSON XIX.

PART I.—PERIODS OF THE HUMAN RACE.

(4) Israel as a Kingdom—Saul to Zedekiah.

God allows his people to "try doing like other people."

Unity.

Under Saul.   Continual War,
I Sam. xiv, 52.
Under David.   Ark brought back,
II Sam. vi, 17.
Under Solomon.   Temple built,
I Kings viii, 63.

Division.

Revolt of Ten Tribes, I Kings xii, 16, 17.
Work of Elijah and Elisha,
I Kings xvii – II Kings xiii.
Jonah's prophesying, Jonah i-iii.

Decay.

Rise of Assyrian Power, II Kings xvii, 4.
Captivity of Ten Tribes,
II Kings xvii, 24.
Captivity of Judah, II Kings xxiv, 12-15.
Isaiah's prophesying.

PRACTICAL THOUGHTS.

Worldly prosperity not permanent,
Prov. xxiii, 5.
Neglect of God brings failure,
II Kings xviii, 11, 12.

PART 2.—DEALING WITH ONE WHO HAS
"TRIED IT ONCE BUT FAILED."

Sin was the cause of failure, Isa. lix, 2.
God offers another opportunity,
Jer. iii, 13, 14; II Cor. ix, 8.

NOTES ON LESSON XIX.

LESSON XX.

PART I.—PERIODS OF THE HUMAN RACE.

(5) The Jewish Province. Cyrus to Herod.

God's people ruled by other nations.

Under Persians.
Temple rebuilt, Ez. i.
Walls rebuilt, Neh. ii-vi.

Under Macedonians.
Palestine made part of Syria.

Under Egyptians.
Septuagint translation of the Old Testament.

Under Syrians.
Jerusalem pillaged.
Jewish religion forbidden.

Under Maccabees.
Struggles for freedom.
Nominal Independence.

Under Romans.
Heavy Taxation, Luke ii, 1.
Herod as King, Matt. ii, 1.

Record for this period chiefly in the first book of the Maccabees and the writings of Josephus.

PART 2.—DEALING WITH ONE WHO THINKS
HIMSELF "AS GOOD AS SOME
CHRISTIANS."

He is measuring himself by the wrong
standard, II Cor. x, 18; Gal. ii, 16.

He is a sinner, Rom. iii, 10.

He cannot get along as well as the
Christian, I Tim. iv, 8; I Pet. iv, 18.

———

NOTES ON LESSON XX.

LESSON XXI.

PÀRT I.—PERIODS OF THE HUMAN RACE.

(6) *The Early Church.*

(a) Ascension of Christ and promise of His return.

God having revealed Himself through Christ, makes the witnesses ambassadors of the gospel.

The Resurrection, Luke xxiv, 1–7.
Stone rolled away.
Linen wraps lying.
Announcement by angels.

Forty Days Interval.
Ten appearances, Matt. xxviii; Mark xvi; Luke xxiv; Jno. xx, xxi; Acts i; I Cor. xv.
To the Women, 2.
To the Disciples, 6.
To others, 2.

The Ascension.
Promise of Power, Acts i, 8.
Taken up in a cloud, Acts i, 9.
Promise of Return, Acts, i, 10, 11.

PRACTICAL THOUGHTS.

Christians to testify the gospel,
Acts ii, 32.
Second coming of Christ the chief comfort for the Christian and greatest motive for active service,
I Thess. iv, 16-18; Luke xix, 13, 15.

PART 2.—DEALING WITH ONE WHO DON'T
WANT TO THINK ABOUT RELIG-
IOUS MATTERS.

He can profit by thinking and acting
now, Deut. xi, 26-28.

The opportunity rejected will not always
remain, Prov. i, 24-26; Isa. i, 28.

NOTES ON LESSON XXI.

LESSON XXII.

PART I.—PERIODS OF THE HUMAN RACE.

(6) *The Early Church.*

b) Holy Spirit Given and Church Founded.

———————

The Holy Spirit.

Descent at Pentecost, Acts ii, 1-4.
Miraculous power given,
Acts iii, 6, 7; v, 12.
Boldness for testimony given,
Acts iv, 8-10, 31, 33.

The Church.

Constituted of Baptized believers,
Acts ii, 41, 42.
Ordination of Deacons, Acts vi, 1 6.
Called Christians, Acts xi, 26.

———————

PRACTICAL THOUGHTS.

The Holy Spirit inspires Mission effort,
Acts i, 8.
Have ye received the Holy Ghost?
The Church loved by Christ, Eph. v, 27.
Do ye also love the Church?

PART 2.—DEALING WITH ONE WHO DON'T BE-
LIEVE IN OUR KIND OF RELIGION BECAUSE
HIS FATHER THINKS EVERYBODY
WILL BE SAVED SOMEHOW.

Show him that his father's belief cannot
answer for him, Rom. xiv, 12.

He must be sure what road he is on,
Prov. xiv, 12.

He can be saved only by forsaking all
sin, Rev. xxi, 27, and being born again,
John iii, 3.

NOTES ON LESSON XXII.

LESSON XXIII.

PART I.—PERIODS OF THE HUMAN RACE.

(6) *The Early Church.*

(c) Spread of Christianity among the Jews. Seven years spent in attempts to to evangelize them.

Persecution.

Peter and John (imprisonment),
Acts iv, 1-4.
Stephen (martyrdom), Acts vii, 57-60.
The Church (scattered), Acts viii, 1-4.

Teaching.

Peter and John in Samaria, Acts viii, 14.
Saul at Damascus, Acts ix, 18-22.
Peter in Lydda, Saron, etc.,
Acts ix, 32-35.

PRACTICAL THOUGHTS.

The benefits of persecution,
Rom. viii, 28.
The duty of Christians to teach others,
I Pet. iii, 15; II Tim. ii, 24, 25.

PART 2.—DEALING WITH ONE WHO DON'T
BELIEVE THERE IS A HELL.

He is deceived,
        Matt. xxiv, 4; II Thess. ii, 11.
Hell is a place of torment,
    .   Luke xvi, 23; Matt. xxv, 41, 46.
Failure to believe a fact does not affect
the fact, Rom. iii, 3.

NOTES ON LESSON XXIII.

LESSON XXIV.

PART I.—PERIODS OF THE HUMAN RACE.

(6) *The Early Church.*

(d) Spread of Christianity among the Gentiles. The Jews rejecting Christ's spiritual reign, its privileges are extended to the Gentiles.

By God's Will.

Revealed to Peter, Acts x.

Revealed to Apostles, Acts xi, 1-18.

Revealed to Jews, Acts xiii, 38-47.

Through Human Means.

Preaching and Miracles,

Acts xiv, 1, 3, 8-10.

Persecution, Acts xiii, 50; xiv, 19,

Elders ordained, Acts xiv, 23.

PRACTICAL THOUGHTS.

God desires all to be saved,

I Tim. ii, 3, 4.

We are to spread the news,

Luke xxiv, 47.

PART 2.—HOW TO TAKE PART IN A MEETING.

(1) Prepare beforehand, II Tim. ii, 15.
(2) Don't be frightened, Jer. i, 8.
(3) Trust in God for strength,
                              Ex. iv. 12.

NOTES ON LESSON XXIV

LESSON XXV.

PART I.—PETER, THE APOSTLE TO THE JEWS.

Meaning of name, Rock.

History.

Son of Jonas, John xxi, 15.
A Fisherman, Matt. iv, 18.
A Married Man, Matt. viii, 14.

Character.

Self-confident, Mark xiv, 29.
Impulsive, Matt. xiv, 29.
Affectionate, John xxi, 17.

Work.

Preaching, Acts ii, 14-36.
Miracles, Acts ix, 32-40.
Writings, I Pet. and II Pet.

PRACTICAL THOUGHTS.

Peter was not a Pope or Mediator,
I Tim. ii, 5.
God's forbearance with weak natures,
Ps. ciii, 14.
We should be active in service,
Eph. vi, 10.

PART 2.—HOW TO LEAD A MEETING.

1.   Get thoroughly into the spirit of the
topic by prayerful study a week or two in
advance.

2.   Arrange all details of the plan, in-
cluding opening talk by leader, short testi-
monies by such others as may be wise,
songs, etc., Ezek. xxxviii, 7.

3.   Be natural.   Don't try to imitate
some other person's manners.

4.   Adhere to the topic.   Plan to interest
the hearers in it.

5.   Be brief: "long talks always exhaust
the time, frequently exhaust the topic and
generally exhaust the audience."

6.   Use popular music that is in har-
mony with the topic, occasionally introduc-
ing some new song, Ps. xxxiii, 3.

7.   Depend upon the Lord for His
blessing.

—————

NOTES ON LESSON XXV.

LESSON XXVI.

PART I.—PAUL, THE APOSTLE TO THE
GENTILES.

Meaning of name, Little.

Preparation, Acts xxii, 3-28.
A Roman, Jew, City Bred.
Educated in Bible Truth.
Converted by Miracle.

Active Work.
Preaching, Damascus, Jerusalem, etc.,
Acts ix, 22-29.
3 Missionary Journeys, Acts xiii-xxi.
Preaching and Teaching at Rome,
Acts xxviii, 16-31.

Writings.
Gospel–Rom., Col., Eph.
Suggestions to Churches,
I Cor., I Tim., Titus.
Concerning Second Coming,
I and II Thess., II Tim.

PART 2.—HOW TO FOLLOW UP A MEETING.

Be armed with *your own Bible* which should be so familiar to you that you can readily find such passages as may be needed.

Be natural in your approach to such as you think have been impressed with the thoughts of the meeting.

Observe the suggestions in Part 2 of Lesson X, and take the name, address, and church preference of the inquirer, to hand to the leader of the meeting or the secretary of the association.

———

NOTES ON LESSON XXVI.

www.ingramcontent.com/pod-product-compliance
Lightning Source LLC
Chambersburg PA
CBHW022033080426
42733CB00007B/822

* 9 7 8 3 3 3 7 1 7 1 6 1 2 *